salmonpoetry

Publishing Irish & International

Poetry Since 1981

Wild, Again
Bertha Rogers

Published in 2019 by
Salmon Poetry
Cliffs of Moher, County Clare, Ireland
Website: www.salmonpoetry.com
Email: info@salmonpoetry.com

ISBN 978-1-912561-41-4

Cover & Title Page Art: *"Treed Fisher with Gold Halo" by Bertha Rogers*
Cover Design & Typesetting: *Siobhán Hutson*

Printed in Ireland by Sprint Print

Salmon Poetry gratefully acknowledges the support of
The Arts Council / An Chomhairle Ealaíon

—to the memory of my husband,
Ernest M. Fishman—

March 19, 1929 – March 16, 2016

Contents

I.

II.

III.

I.

This dissolving of the evenings is still ours.

—from "Indian Serenade"
by Eugenio Montale

HOLY BEAST

Once I was part of a holy beast, I *was*.
I was a dog, a bear, a horse.
I was the leader and the dragging-led.

My fur was both sleek and shaggy, black and white.
I was as tall as a stallion, long-maned,
yet bony, as deep withered as a dog.

I barked and I whinnied, I growled.
I cantered and I loped, I lumbered.

This was before I was born, before I slid
from the cave, where I was hailed
then demeaned for my unnatural cries.

I rose up—red dog spinning rain, swirling
band of pink. At last they knew me in my corner.
The words they gave left. I barked again.

TO THE HEART

I have taken up residence in the bear's
black body; the bear's heart has devoured
mine. I (all my thumping) am diminished.
And the bear grows bigger; his seething face
has absorbed all the day's light, his clawed paws
are as turbulent as electricity at night.
Heart, the sunflowers have been extinguished
by hurled rays, and I am dead to the day.

They told me I would discover morning,
but here it is always night, though the walls
be red and flowing (blood moves,
genome-smart but knowing not of itself,
all its bodies sequenced and thwarted
though paginated, booked, and shelved).

The bear refuses to read the pages I was.
Spits me out. The blinded blinds move
like flattened smiles in air's carried currents.
Crows pick out, lay down words between
light's molten lines. *Never forget you!*
Never forget your thronged face, they cry.
The bear is silent, his viral eyes red-hot.

BLUE BEAK SPEAKING

The apothecary door mirrors need,
images yourself conspired from nothing.

You are a dog, a wolf, a coyote
Your under-face waits.

That physician in the reflection
a walking smile. *It's world-death,*

his wide teeth intone, *these open*
sores disease's beginning.

Plead. No answers are given
the smile laughs, white coat swaying.

You mark seasons in your head.

In the forest, a crow's wings rent
from torso, scattered over dry needles.

Someone, something, anyone's game.
Nearby, Crow's skull shows on duff,

eye holes watch, jaw hinges, a maw
and blue-black, that beak speaks.

Your talons, a twig, raise beak up.
You, like Crow, position it with

precision. This is the truth of it
physician's killer yap, *yapping.*

You are change, you the canid you,
only this lonely morning, reflected.

HAWK'S REASON

When the hawk leaves his tree for movement
among the green, when he aims earthward,
the air opens for him as if sliced by a deft
knife, space disappearing into time's
aperture. The nosing gray vole, knowing she
will cease, sharply screams, screams twice.

The hawk flexes lightning-bright talons;
his wings broadcast intent; close and break
like thunder, dimming June's new blades.

When the hawk's blazing claws wreathe
the vole's rolling body, his gleaming beak
arcs toward the fleet heart, and blood's first,
deepest drop drops through blue—
the whole sky opens, blameless and distinct.

STONE AND STAND

First, I was mountain, one among
many—our shoulders shoved up, rough.
We jostled and pushed, seeking blue;
we grew meager from the ceaseless
butting, our borders rupturing,
rounding down to stippled smallness.

Then I was stone, alone. I stood
in a green field, below a flimsy sky.
I was hugely still. There was quiet
around, within—just air and I.

In time, faces with voices showed—
limbs, hands. Grunting, they hoisted
my bulk. I said nothing, pondered
where they would, at last, set me down.

They broke me, they piled me up
with my kind. Now we rest, together,
screened by trees who seeded themselves
in our abraded bodies, thin skin—
those high, shifting limbs ours, too.

We are become a host, yet one—
rooted, riveted. Fingered arms
sign our big thoughts in air, but we
hold; stillness is our wary way.
We are grove, and we slowly think—
slow we go, back—from stand, to range.

PLANTING WILDNESS

The stooped and swaying labor
that planted a thousand seedling
spruces is not wasted; immediately

they take to the mountain. In
seven days, and as if they were native
to this thin earth, they display

bright, wild needles from the tips
of their fingers. While
you wane, the trees increase,

their bodies adding arms, adding
digits. In ten years they attain
a giant's height. Fifteen years,

and there is no trace of the meadow
that tried to choke their roots;
the sun's light cannot penetrate

their density. Birds nest, bears
test their circumference. You,
remembering the old, tamed slope,

avert your eyes as you enter;
walk cautiously among spiraling
branches. This is the reason you

lift your head off the pillow
each morning, you go willing
to sleep every night. Even when

the bleakness is hard upon you.

WILD, AGAIN

When the forest was field, after
orchard (after field, after forest),
when these spruces had not been thought
by grasses encumbered only
by wild red strawberries;
the dogs ran in there, every day—
they corralled and cowed speckled Ayrshires,
whooped and barked for their farmer-lords.
They herded those cows to stalls—
until the milk was gone, the barns fell down.

Then there was a rainy planting—
fingerlings slippered into bladed
soil; rocked, clayed soil—followed
by slow growth, passage to sky's eye,
patient, steady renovation
from green staves, red fruit, earth's increase,
to stippled, needled, knotty ground.

And, at last, only this slant-lit
site where primal dog-paws pound russet
spurs shed by leaning, lithe under-boughs.
Ah! Wind soughing, susserating—
and just there, the doe's immigrant
eyes—home, again, in her found wild.

THE OLD DOG'S LAMENT

I.

I was barking all the time when
I was a pup. I couldn't get
enough of the sound of my high
vagabond voice, the parallel
report from the ridge-scraped barn,
glaciated pond. The turtle,
even the heron stopped to hear
my song! I was a blithe boy!

And those days spun out, unbroken.
Then I met the yellow bitch with
the feral smell, exhorting voice.
She and I—we became one beast,
our fur commingling on the hill,
mouths eating wind, feet in tandem.

II.

Even after, coming to see
my sweet in that last place—splayed and
spread where she found her end (I could
barely suss her fur there, dead, grayed
among last summer's sere stems),
her smell still lay, heavy, on the hay.
I had jaw-dragged her after
the tire's bump and thud, listened as
she whimpered her awful death.
But I could not stop her going.

No one has to tell me to cease
my sorrow-song. I carry her face
behind my eyes, now and then lift
my head at what I recollect—
her bark, joy-struck eyes, tail thrilling
against our days' blue, blue skies.

DOG GIRL DISCUSSES TRANSFORMATION

Nothing mattered
anymore, even though the moon
was as full as a drunk's face,
even though the stars still shone.
Your body hung above
the low grass, wafted among
waving green blades, feet
quiet, an unclocked creature's.
It was then—
you noticed that the black cat had
gone, the cat had disappeared,
the cat was no more—
even as your own eyes
tilted and your nose twitched,
your nails curved and climbed.
You were alone
in your night, and at last it
was June, always June.

LUNA

Luna, I have longed to see you, touch your
creamy green wings. Wanted your eyes on *me*,
false romancer! Oh, I stopped for the hawk
moth, dazzled by his hummingbird buzz, needling
beak—how he throbbed over the purple phlox's
honey! I summoned my husband, our guests,
pointed out the insect's antics. August thrummed
around us. Enough? Should have been, like
the day I made this drawing of my left hand,
trembling beneath the maple's leaves, awaiting
that summer's lover. Ancient heat, long ago.
I am and am not sorry. I still desire
the translucent luna, his arrayed rings—
nothing can diminish my need for green.

BLUE JAYS IN SEPTEMBER WINDOW

Window cranked, window half-open,
watery glass eyeing sere September grasses,
blades fading through cracked window,
foxtails outside, dead in clumps.

Blue Jays are screeching morning,
but crows are quiet, civil—blue is stronger
here, jays' bright blue. Jays' wings serrate
the lapis atmosphere, floating leaves.
They tumble, flit, flourish beyond
apples, falling pears—they are true sky.

Now the crows begin, more persistent
than jays—bigger, louder, their grief wide
open, like autumn windows to cyan sky.
A blood-red cardinal sinks into fall's
last branches, its *pretty pretty* tipping,
spilling into wrecked, blue-red sumac.

NIGHT AND LOOSESTRIFE

This sequence begins before anyone wakes.
Yes, it is the dark of night, and the walls
have closed their eyes. The pillow speaks
of other heads, altruistic dreams; the pillow
is bent on spilling all its pledged secrets.

I, too, may choose to disclose many enigmas,
the black dress, flowing over the chair's
slender ebony arm, scornfully reports,
I chiefly enjoy trapping evil in my seams.

The keys in their deep pocket clatter, ring,
discuss other doors. I? I cannot move, neither
more nor less; I am held in place by staid and
relentless coverlets. The loosestrife just outside
my window, lazy in its deep ditch, has traveled
a long way; it journeys by itself and in packs,
its pretty pink dress enough of a reason.

NOTE: Loosestrife is an invasive plant in America, growing
and overtaking native flowers.

ORIOLE

She is too old. The last orange bird has flown
to the center of the earth—once, and for all.
Alone in her heart, she is without heart.
Yet the sun rises and shines; the warbling
oriole, its feathers flaring fast—orange
against rapt black, song stretching spring
to summer—becomes summer. She is old.
The feather on the forest floor, glister-
planchette pointed toward Earth's core, trembles
among last October's left leaves. The feather
wishes to fly again, bear her body
to the nest, the heart-hole of darkest Earth.
The feather takes her there and, though she is
too old, she is, at last, for now, content.

STONE COLD

Knew I was finished, *did* I, when didn't
recall the oriole's seasonal notes,
orange flash over stone, when too grail-gone to
discern words. Faulty rightness had taken me
over then, torched all the blue-white houses,
charred their closed eyes. And all I gleaned was one
flawed axiom. Sooth! Would my *Was*, my *Did*,
in the fullness of stones, be lofted, cleansed?
Hill pinnacle—not one tree, buoyant leaf.
There arranged my menhirs as if they were
dancing hags, two-steps stringent as Christians'.
They cajoled, old stones, but I would not fuse
with them, knew I wanted shadow more than flash.
Showed valley to the ladies. *Did*. They gave up.

THE BITCH PROTESTS
LITTER MURDERS

When I was a singer of rain-dark songs,
I stood beneath important coats and gowns
and opened my throat, and the notes fell out,
and stroked those fabled jackets, sleek silks.

All the lights dimmed then, as though to hide
mayhem, and the suits and dresses fixed
their eyes on laden tables, and cried.

When I saw their tear-streaked faces,
heard their chiasmic moans, I spun on my
padded soles; escaped to righteous fields.

Teats leaking, womb aching, I disdained
their breached, lying grief,
even their own, howling offspring's—

I wept instead for my own kind, my doomed
daughters, gunny-sacked, drowned in the deeps,
by the farm's calloused, practiced grasp.

BOY WITH .22

The boy aims; shoots.
The flourishing squirrel
leaches blood
like the leaves he enters.

The flourishing squirrel.
His feather tail floats high
like the leaves he enters,
the dying grasses in the ditch.

His feather tail floats high;
nailed feet breach star stream,
the dying grasses in the ditch.
The rodent's eyes stare at fire;

nailed feet breach star stream;
cry hushed in falling snow.
The rodent's eyes stare at fire;
he understands: the season wants him

hushed in falling snow,
his darkened, sharp, bone blades.
He understands: the season wants him,
the weight he used to bear.

His darkened, sharp, bone blades,
entropy's wintry wings;
the weight he used to bear
in spring, vanishing like snow in sun.

Entropy's wintry wings
discretely wave to green
in spring. Vanishing, like snow in warmth,
grasses widen in summer, burgeon

discretely, wave to green.
Braiding disheveled bones,
grasses widen in summer, burgeon.
Autumn happens again,

braiding disheveled bones.
Growth erodes like shot;
autumn happens again
to the same, spent squirrel.

Growth erodes like shot,
crowded grains, fallen eye arch.
To the same spent squirrel,
earth's one promise.

Crowded grains, fallen eye arch—
death's worn truth—
earth's one promise
over and again.

Death's worn truth:
the boy aims, shoots,
over and again,
leaches blood.

WANT

I wanted to be one, complete—
a manuscript illuminated,
swarming with answers—wanted
my spine to be sewn and strung,
flat-faced, as if bound by Copts,
so that those who lifted my cover
would see all clearly—no gutter secrets,
just words and pictures of trees
standing in high-grassed, green fields.
I wanted those old pages to scud
like winded clouds, tear like dogs
careering after rabbits through
tired pastures—no dens, no pock-
marked, scarred grounds to outsmart
any reader. I wanted it all open—
and only the rabbits screaming.

RAVENS

I. Ravens, Solstice

Raven on winter branch.
Snow skidding blind windows.
I am alone, the poem flown
to the crown of the tallest tree.

No. I am with my poem;
we are cryptic as a raven's corpse,
punctuated by one black beard.

We ascend, and I find I was deluded—
we are two ravens, not words,
one holding on, one dropping,
plummeting, then rising, and aloft,
become counterfeit canticle—
or are we flux, waiting;
brilliance, kindled?

In my cottage, the sound
of shingles shrugging off grizzled husks—
fresh tumult, croaked motifs.

II. Ravens, the Autumn Equinox

The time I saw the raven on the fir—
the very top, where no needles put forth—
the sky was coherent,

jay blue before night's mean weather—
that was the moment belief seized me.
And that dense juncture
should have been sufficient.

But then—and this is tangled—
the raven winched his beard forward,
broadened his Stygian wing,
and morphed into—two.

I stood, stilled, as those birds undid creed.
I didn't struggle, did not spar;
no, I let doubt abrade my face.

That time, now and again,
beats in me like confounded wings—
what have I thrown away;
                              what lost?

MORNING, OCTOBER: THE STONE CIRCLE

Who stands in this October meadow
stands for grass, for bending heads
of goldenrod. Her weather side accepts
southerly wind, distant dark cancelling
clouded crests. She answers the circled
horizon, finally holding in her mind
the all-whirling world. The upright
walker, now halted, is pleased to back-
drop kneeling blades while stones tilt
to receive sun, its blue-eyed sky
slashed by rays and scratched black
trees, haloed limbs now left by leaves.
She is pleased to burden grassed ground;
receive the gathering, building, risen
breeze. With all her fingers she grips
morning's grave breath, holds in that
warm room the everyday, blinding day.

FORTUNE

Here I am, November, inside your vague weather—
fog drift swaying vision, slouching on my chest.

Up the branched slope, atop the black spruces,
crows raucously claim ownership of this land.

In another country, that November, clouds surrounded
the train I rode past crowded mountain tracts.

I was *there*, believer, a bear burning for this real
future, this hollowed old apple, dug-out den—

I was learning how to lay down my head.

BOGUS

When snow's pointed stars embrace
this unbalanced earth,
when that cold stuff warms
its own particles—
answers, driven by wind,
arrive in storms—.
And the mind clears,
each eye a cyclop's, every aspect curved,
each black tree gliding
in old concentric circles,
Sufi-ecstatic, leaves easing like fingers
from perfectly round fruit
to open mouths, taking up the task.
It's always this way,
no matter the bogus warmth of October.

FALL

I stumbled. Dropped into the cold of old
December. Fell, and didn't care one bit.
Wished to be wed to the coyote barking
his sorry song. Renounced all my so-far
days, straddled road's yellow, then watched
the space where I stood vanish. Then I yawped,
Take me, not the calf so recently birthed,
not the lamb, precipitously exposed. Waited.

No word. I picked myself up; ran toward
the rogue's cry, conceding all my martyred
tomorrows. *What the hell*, I laughed; and died
laughing, proof that I was in a fit state,
corroboration that my epoch had *been*.
Stretched out, ecstatic. I was cold, *for good*.

THE DAY

December faces smiling beneath long-grassed ground,
all together—homing, mouths mouthing—
Say, stay, no need to fly on ravens' wings.

Sudden, that white-speared grin bright-rising.
(It wants brindled pinions, guide-wings,
desires other mysteries, broad-feathered fun.)

Sun's slant spectral, snow slipping down,
whirling above evening-layered macadam.
Green red yellow blades, Solstice's haze-change.

Shadows slide, overtake all color when the god
looses his thrice-shaped, black bolt
and autumn's last silent space, leaning face glows

like a needled compass in a winter woods.
The lost dog dry-noses down to lost thoughts—
Do not want to leave. My heart swells.

But those black birds lift, they send every notion home.

AT SOLSTICE

1.

Earth takes back her color.
The limbs of trees, bleak
as buzzards' wings, truthful
as old bones, rake the sky.
The pond is grave-numb;
the wind, all arrows.

2.

The moon, wearing a milky nimbus,
wreathes the East.

Out of the biting dark—
Light, shining.

HIGHWAY IN WINTER

Bitter blue noon; I driving, doubled, twice
helixed; I'm my own mobius, spiraled
DNA. This road—cold gray corpse turned
inside out, car riding its frozen wave.
Tomorrow is always last August, last year.
Tomorrow I raised my daughters and they,
other-eyed, begat me. Next week I married
8 men, murdered them in their pillared beds,
serially. Not sorry, sorry no more—
not last month, when I was 80, nor now
that I am 18, breasts birthing, become
8, drowned again; then new, whelped from freezing
fluid. The mountains, eroding, rising,
agree with the w(8)ted odometer.

II.

I grew up where all was patterned and silent. . .

—from "The Willow" by ANNA AKHMATOVA

CLOSING

—for Ron Guichard

Today I said yes to the land.
In the presence of witnesses I took
up my pen and pressed

its fine point to documents.
Today I married earth, wood, and
stone. The surveyor's circles

mark my land's extremities on a sky
as clear as June's. The garden's
cleanly white; the lilac

patterns her shape on the snow—
all those fingers scratching
through winter! Down

the road starlings dance
on the backs of sheep; wild turkeys
whirl out of the forest.

The mountains, rearing up,
burn blue. Earth's ancestors
open her door to me.

The well shudders and coughs up
the same sweet water I remember
from another, flatter life.

This is that life, elevated to clouds,
this is the land in the sky I miraged
out of black canyons.

TWO WINTER RONDEAUS

1. *First Day*

I wake to the new year's low-rolling morning, its dead stars.
Dawn's wind scourges the horizon, lashes hawthorn limbs.
All night, wild animals shambled past my sight. Now,
scars on new snow—mouse tracks, halted; an owl pellet.
Beneath the grizzled pine, fanned-out, shattered ferns:

generations of deer rested here, four of them, together.
A jay strikes the quiet above the frozen pond. I walk out
on the white, try to extract a gnarled bough from a crack.
I wake to the new year's low-rolling morning, its dead stars

breaking my heart. What if I said there were no more
hours; what if, in the dream I dream, the ice crazed around
its cold old stick?—. The moon tilts loudly. My boots lurch
into black. From my throat, a flooded language.
Nothing comes near; no one quits drifts to listen.
I wake to the new year's low-rolling morning, its dead stars.

2. After Blizzard

A single vehicle skids the road.
The wind has died. Lights roll, cold,
like owls' eyes in blackened woods.
Night gives over to misunderstood
light. You used to read each day's code,

used to dream of the next abode,
next life, reversing all you ever owed.
You were younger, you felt good.
Storms were different then—

they were beautiful, they flowed.
Now you are end-directed, old,
now there's only chopped wood
to warm the noisy furnace. No good
here, nothing but the day, uncontrolled.
Storms were different, then.

OLD JANUARY

Out of somewhere we don't know comes less than
zero. This shrouded hour is so cold that
coyotes quiet among the Cimmerian
spruces they call home; mountains crack open.

This is how it ends—world warmed, wrought so
by our hectic hands; ice born of hordes;
inside-out weather. The spent planet freezes
bodies off its grated curves while they sleep.

It's four in the morning; this day will fall
further, then ordain a swathed sun. All
feathers will shiver and stiffen, all song
will cease. We protest; we have done no wrong.

WOLF MOON

Two days past full.
The wolf eyes
February's glassy snow.
Above his listening head
Orion's sword anchors
the southern sky;
Sirius limns boundary trees.

A low growl—a plane
speeding east, breaching quiet.
The sky grows teeth
in her black face.

I have set my yellow chair here,
at world's end;
here, take my meals.
My tongue rests
on the bottom of my mouth:
stone thawed,
stone drinking stars,
the barked light.

SAP MONTH

The clouds, sleet-laden, shift.
The ridge moves. I am going right out,
                                        into it.

                    Sky; I am sky; I lie along the horizon,
trees black against cloudy body.
                    I am, O! coming down, clearing.

                                              Floor;
I, gray stone mother; red hummock-chair,
white veins on stone face, snow.
I am spectrum; I proclaim
                    Day.

Coyote stares; eyes, teeth, yellow.
                              Shadbush strains
from frozen earth.
                    Maple waits; pulp, blood, ready.

Doglike, I scratch my belly and yawn.
          Warmth happens to my body; my teeth fang.

                    From this moment heat beats forth,
these wan hours are charged.

                    I waft through limpid air;
spirit in the very old air, feather up
to green sky–
                    O! my head is jay-proud.

I cry.
       Sun,
             I say,
                        bloom again.
          Come,
               bring me

                    to your glare.

AFTER WATCHING THE DEER
IN THE TREES

Before you grasped the Creator's ruthlessness
you saw yourself devout as a Jain, feet
floating over grass, not bruising, not bending;
and the plants, in return, causing no hurt.
Your body is heavier than your faith
yet the flowers you trample revive
daily. Who permits the beaver to gnaw
the tree's heart withdraws just as the woman
in the corner crooks her arm, shields her face
from exploding fists. Broken, she lies down
no more, no less than her tormentor. Havoc
waits; the deer silently leaps. Then winter
returns, its horizon blurring branches.

TREED FISHER

I hang on, sway and pitch—
leaf curving, turning in wind,
nailed hands clamping branch.

I, foul cloud, in and out of fear—
I glare down at the beasts
who barked me, treed me.

Fiercest in the forest,
I scrabbled up this gale-roost
where blackbirds pivot and swivel,

explain my place to me.
I will stay, hold my own
until Sky shuts his seeing-eye,

and those rabble-dogs
whirl into night's door light.
If I were back on my earth,

I would incise my line in dirt.
I would lunge, rip, bite, gnaw.
But I am detained; day glow grips me.

Those eager ones, teeth clacking,
dancing, hope my hold to loosen,
hope my end to bring.

Still I bide. I will ess down
this rough pole, find my way
back to wild, weasel among

stumps, rotting hollows—
my own, welcome home.

NOTE: The fisher (Pekania pennanti) is a fierce mammal
(member of the mustelid family, native to North America).

ON NORTH MOUNTAIN

That bone-wrenching,
wood-racking,
crashing—
and coming there,
face wreathed in green,
ears trailing twigs;
standing *here*—Bear.

She shows,
feral sister—
tree-tall, leaf-dappled—
feeble eyes staring,
scent-informed.

She blazes a trail
that isn't there,
a deception from beginning
to circling end; she
tramples flowers and fungi—
the red toadstool,
bitten like wisdom's apple,
a clue.

Down she drops,
black storm raging
within the tangle;
and her sable children—
secret no more—
Byzantine-spiral
up the birch's white body.

Again she flashes—
deep death medicine—
then miracles away,
north and to the east.

FOX ON VOLCÁN IRAZÚ, COSTA RICA,

She crosses the path,
in her mouth a mouse.
This crater at the very top
of the shrouded world is hers.
Her babes are hungry,
and the towering creatures before her falter,
so why not dawdle.

She's shown herself
near the umbrella plants, just south
of flowers that blossom and halt.
She doesn't know that her own footing
will vent and gush, again,
its seething green lake
drowned by exploding stone.

She steps out, hardly marking
the two women watching,
listening to the lone junco's acrid chirp.
She's blending,
coat flecked like lava rock.
The mouse spasms.

NOTE: The active volcano, 11,260 feet high, last erupted in 1963.

COMPENSATION

Because you and I will never be bird,
because we will never, glancing downward,
lift furled arms, invent wings; never tuck
taloned pins under feathered tail, nor feel
the slipstream against flensed eyes; nor know the close
admiration of sun against clouds' supple
surfaces; the safety of plumes in rain—

we must cultivate a quiet contentment,
be pleased to bask in each other's riffling
gaze, tease each other's hands with opulence;
we must adore the feel of foot on soil,
slow satisfaction of gravity, touch
of lips to lips—not, *yet*, the beak's sharp steel.

THE PEAR TREE

Say that, while blading the plant-trench, you
saw leaves before they pushed out. As you
angled the sapling's feet into soil, booted
earth over roots, you tasted the fruit,
catalog's promise years mere minutes.

This summit home, where you the living
try to thrive among stones exposed, deprived
of soil this site wants five seasons before
it allows the tree fruit. Then, and at last,
the tree is pear-heavy not the golden,
smooth, shining sugar you visioned
but mottled, mildewed, misshapen eggs.

Say you, lost planter, watch while the deer,
the weather reap ground-crop mush
among freezing fall, fungus-fingered leaves.

From the porch that holds your feet to
this home, you recall all the other children
you failed, every garden you let go.

COPPER BEECH TREES IN WINTER

Leaves arc, like paintings of blown leaves;
like cut paper, like sunset strewn
across red-gold sky, like smoldering fires;

serrate-edged, notched, like some knives.
But they cut only the hard wind,
the wind that tries to bridge them.

Wind can't; these trees are too feisty;
they do not hide in niches or ditches;
they flaunt, they claim rough edges.

Farmers name beeches weeds; they push
through field soil. Their roots patiently wait,
shove worker-laid stones, open faces.

December disrupts, beats black branches,
feathered, fingered twigs; they're like pens
writing winter's aggregate history;

black barriers; hinged nodes above snow,
hanging on against blizzard breath;
hanging on all the scarred, bleak season.

SEASON

Last summer every tomato
vine birthed her own offspring. Deer stepped
amid the green, low moon lighting
their tract, hooves embossing earth.
Blunt teeth bit into the fat red
globes, each fruit a present complete.
Cauliflower blossomed beyond
green buds, blew up to yellow, and
lost her name to autumn's hurled leaves,
hard wind. The deer, glutted, content,
wind rousing fur, raised russet
heads, spun back into black woods. And
then the moon made off, its wide bowl
depleted. Winter happened, white
drifts austere yet blooming in cold's
cramped fingers. By and by they all slept.

SAVAGE

White teeth. Hands, fright-gliding the dusk.
His fingers lift your shirt from your waist,

displacing folds of fabric.
Eyes inscrutable, silken jacket shifting,

he could be the robed mandarin
you always imagined—intelligent, perfidious.

You expect a tale of intrigue but he lifts
your chin to thin lips, silent.

Elegant fingers map your skin,
stacked back bones; fluent hands trouble

the bones while storied mouth shapes words.
The sun has gone to sleep,

the moon a heated disk. Feet struggle
in rotting leaves. You are as young

as you were, tender figure slammed
against hard car door, white blouse torn.

Your sleeves ribbon the tepid air
like a flock of birds hesitating to migrate.

The trees say nothing. Your eyes take in
the plush front seat, turned wheel, jet glass.

The moon displays your return.
That which had been concealed shows,

like the face of a corpse found floating
in tranquil waters, like a hand

instinctively warding off the blow.
The dog waits by the door, the dog barks

but, O!—no one but the wind
crossing the palms of leaves. You see.

The mist exposes one branch suspended
as though painted on scrolled silk.

Pictures you can't read texture the sky.
There is nothing, you say, but the thickness

of time. You may disappear; speak constantly
and calmly in a liquid voice, words

as resonant as a heart beating through skin.
Hands will thrust through your face.

How many, you ask, Whose?

DRAGONFLY

I sensed you in the shadows;
your wings worked, summoned
me through congested streets.

Yours was the face bemused
by the glass-reflected sky;
those were *your* faceted eyes
proclaiming pain—
beautiful magnification,
iridescent in the afternoon,
your needling body
green as emeralds spilled
from some god's careless hand
to the city's floor—
where I happened
to be standing, awaiting you.

I turned you over:
  Do you look at me!

I cradled you, jewel creature,
like a dying king
on a catafalque; carried
you to the weed patch.

You hesitated; disengaging,
you reeled among the leaves,
flashing blue, then green
in the late light.

Dreamer! I loved you—
and, loving, left.

BUCK

August: the final Sabbath, the cherished
mountain. Against a blowzy full moon,
an array of antlers. Incautiously

I approached. The buck bent
one startled leg. I stepped harder,
summer's grasses riffling and breaking

beneath my sandals. The buck swung
his wild grave head and broke: earth
thundered, dead stems shaking. I

followed but he traveled too far.
I turned and maundered below, along
the armored garden, its brocade of
beets

and chard, rustling dry vines; into
the tame yellow eyes of the house.
The next night I tried again; lay

myself on the deer's own slope,
in the moon's steady beam; waking,
waking to the flawless circle. At

times, a star punctured the vault.
The buck avoided the terrain.
September's sky: moonless, with wind,

rain-precursing, percussive wind.

SOUTHERLY

I saw it—the dog star—waiting for me,
panting to go forth in the night.
But I was held by hall light,
my body tilting forward,
feet stuck to floor boards
that shifted like sylvan breaths.
They must have remembered
the forest that birthed them,
blades that severed them.
I could do nothing but wait.
The garden below shimmered
like the moon's Lake of Dreams—
this night's meager gift.
Then that dog ran without barking
toward other stars, and I was alone, again.

THREE FOR SUMMER'S END

1. Whale Season*

The moon, a becalmed boat.
In the southeastern sky
the monster's tail bobs,
his head crowned
by fitful stars. Earth's
ocean expands, contuses
layers of sun.

Waves of blood and light
—day start,
rehearsal for season's end.

2. At the Pond Early, with the Dog

We have disturbed the ducks,
the great blue heron.
We have altered
their morning. Now
silence belongs to us.

The trees,
like longtime lovers,
turn in on themselves.

*The constellation Cetus (the whale) is prominent in the
later summer sky.

3. Evening on the Rise

The yellow moon rolls
past day. Moisture weights
the meadow grasses.
The landscape
—an ashy blur,
light's ghost.

Mother Night, the moon
is full; do not ask me
to be born again.

WORK SESTINA

When, at the sun's last reddening, the farmer
unbends from wide and lonely fields,
then relinquishes dead sickled grasses
she has built into softly-snaked mounds,
her ancestors ponder the gift. They climb
the faces of the vaulted barrows

they built long ago. Shaking off the barrows'
yellow threads, past work of the farmer,
the dead, their waists waving, climb
the shorn, compliant fields.
Those dead pause at the mounds
their descendant newly made, grasses

she cut. They part and kneel in grasses,
nodding at the edge of quiet barrows,
their shoulders like spreading mounds.
Streaming behind the farmer,
her spent back, their shrouds scenting fields,
the farmer's dead anxiously climb

the evening's shaft; together they climb,
their addled words parching grasses.
Only the wind in the fields,
the living advise; *those tending the barrows,*
someone calling the hungry farmer,
someone raking the mounds

of the gathering. From heaped mounds
the dead harvest long strands to climb
their tapestried walls. They petition the farmer
to join them in the easy plaiting of grasses,
the braiding of silk for the barrows
they love. *Gold*, they plead, our *golden fields*

are lush, coins adorn our brazen fields.
They show the woman the mounds
she made, guide her stout body toward barrows.
The dead tell how to escape daily labor, climb
down, at last, the whirling, tattered grasses,
believe in rest: *You must leave the farmer*

life, crave barrows for home. You must climb
down fields forever promised to mounds,
grasses enfolding your face, they say, no longer farmer.

WRONG WAY

—*Hawthornden Castle, Midlothian, Scotland*
—*If he comes suddenly
he must not find you asleep . . . keep awake.*

—Mark 13:36-37

Even in that hoary castle
her eyes wanted open windows, unpeopled air—
but her bed faced the wrong way,
faced a fire that, kindled, kinescoped the ceiling—
where she saw a far-off forest
in a long-ago movie, quaveringly ablaze.

> *Who was that boy?
> Whose arm meandered my shoulder,
> fingers entwined mine?
> What technicolor covenant, breached,
> brought me from that lost place
> to another century, another land?*

All through the waxed and waning moon,
the dying fire's parade of trees, she craved sleep.
The window angled the wrong wall;
the chimney howled its nightly offices.

> *I recalled joy—
> his happy traveling hands,
> stay-at-home smile.*

At last she heard something rasp
the well's secret passage;
sensed hands, hand over hand,
to ledge, and down, across glittery grass;
up my wall, feet spidering dressed stones—

and blue fingers clasped and hindered her flesh;
tattooed arms toted her body
to dovecots far below stacked floors where,
broken-necked bird, she lay, eye astare.

     O God, want bared.

Then hands seized her belly—
skin and fat—twisted and wrung the mass,
matter of fact, like a below-stairs servant
extracting water from mop to bucket.

So she was taken,
each coiled night, to that aged galaxy;
so filled the margins of her pages
with heathens scaling forests,
reaching her illuminated chamber.

     *Are **these** the god*
     you desire to believe in,
     this*, the one?*

A wide hand measured her worth.

At moon's end
she left, found her own home again,
but each dusk, without exception,
that palpable apparition collected her flesh.

Where did he go, that one?
What god does he love?
O discomfort, I pray;
O Lord, I want; I will, I swear.

And watch and swear—
all visions ended,
all past and future experience diminished.

NOTE: Hawthornden Castle, built on a sandstone cliff plunging 200 feet to the River Esk, in the Midlothian region of Scotland, is noted for its network of 4th Century, Pictish caves below it. The small castle was begun in the 11th century, with rebuilding taking place in the 15th and 17th centuries. William Drummond, the Scottish poet, owned the castle. Today it is a retreat for writers.

TWO IN WINTER

I.

The horizon, uncertain
this morning;
the landscape,
a Chinese painting:
mountains line up, push
together; the sun
           falls
from their shoulders
into the curving arms
of valleys.

II.

Last night the wind,
loving the house, embraced
her corners.
Last night the wind was happy,
the whole house sang.

VULTURES

From my chair,
at the outer edge of sight,
I see the monster's wings
rocking up the thermals
over the meadow.

When I bend
to the garden and the dog barks,
I look up, to the right:
yes, I see it,
the wrinkled red neck.

Twice, while driving,
I've come upon one undressing
the dead,
its smartly-styled beak
silently slashing.

And several times,
two or three gathered together,
lancing the periphery
of vision. Mesmerized
as a disciple, I follow.

I can't fall asleep
after this shuddering lovemaking;
I get closer, they
hiss and disrobe me
all through the night.

ON THE ROAD

This owl raptured after this muskrat,
seized, ripped off, this bony November day,
the water rat's greasy head.

> *And did the rat grasp what great angel*
> *had taken his body up*
> *eyes riding past hooked blue beak,*
> *beneath roof arched like a church's,*
> *and down mortality's red craw?*

A car, wheeling south, completed the act,
ravished the owl right out of light.

Better than sex, this aborted hunt,
more satisfying than owning the wish, granted love,
the diurnal abuses wreaked upon each other.
Better than mercy; better, balancing all,
this blinding end, glinting, quick death.

RIME

The elements have forgotten themselves
again—the wind, this May, belongs to March,
and morning's frost, to October; rain stings,
like November's. And there has been snow,
the green lawns of spring sprinkled with almost
false flakes. We—actors, all of us—pretend
shock, say *the wind goes right through*, as if we'd
never felt this cold, this time of year.

Truly, we speak of seasons when we mean
without desire, talk of leaves only
when we require nothing. Truly, we
can't love, anymore, the look of rime.
Isn't it, then, *time* to leave this roaring
circle, bright ball of torment? Walk right *off*?

III.

We must learn from it, as far as possible, why, when, and how beauty appears. . .

—from *The Sense of Beauty*
by GEORGE SANTAYANA

THE CAT IN THE DINER

swerves under my table.

I am not surprised.
The prescription for my new glasses
is wrong: surfaces become colors
moving silently past my face,
walls warp at a glance.

The villagers are calm.
They talk among themselves
while mountains tilt at their town.

I eat my lunch,
reach to pet the stray vision.

WALNUTS

Just came in from planting twenty-five black walnut whips on my Catskill mountain—I'm doing it in increments because it's too much to plant all one hundred at once. Swinging the mattock in the sun, the mid-May wind breathing over the rise, I know I'm doing big work—someday, where this glacial meadow waved, a walnut grove will burgeon, its trees wide and tall. Someday, a few generations from now, a woman will ramble among these trees, swinging a galvanized bucket, a receptacle for the wrinkled black nut casings she gathers from October's fallen leaves; she will toss them into the bucket and they will clatter and ban, like hail or thunder, like prodigious rain on roofs.

When I designed *King Lear* in Berkeley in the Seventies, the sound man and I fabricated a thunder machine; we punched random holes in a three-by-four metal sheet, then hung the metal from the light booth ceiling. Gripping the bottom and flexing the sheet, we created the illusion of a rumbling sky, an assault against the old man and his cohorts. Walnuts in their tough husks, shaken in a sap pan, would have done.

These black walnuts, when they are grown, will manufacture juglone, a chemical so toxic that it restricts the growth of other plants; a remembered defense against competition in the wild. It is for this reason that I plant the trees far from my flower and vegetable garden. The scientists at the DEC recommend planting walnut trees in rows, alternating with cardinal autumn olives. The olive trees, growing quickly, keep grasses down while allowing the immature walnuts to thrive. In a few years the olives are sacrificed to the walnuts' superior stamina and poisonous emissions. I like autumn olives, so my walnuts will slowly make it on their own.

Black walnuts (in primordial times growing to one-hundred fifty feet) are an upper story, "climax" species in their original state. Long lived and deeply rooted, they are also drought-resistant. Leonardo ground the hulls for pigment but, although just the touch of them stains hands and clothing, the hue didn't endure in his works. The wood is valued for fine furniture and pianos; its grain is close, its color a rich and congenial purplish brown that takes a French polish well. In fifty or one hundred years, someone, cutting my trees for lumber, could become wealthy.

Just north of the woodshed, on the Iowa farm where I was raised, there was a huge black walnut tree. Playing "King on the Mountain," a knoll of corncobs, we aimed the pod-heavy harvest at each other in the fall. We cracked the shells in winter, to make fudge and penuche. One year, at the edge of the lawn, a walnut volunteered to grow. *The squirrel must have forgotten it*, Dad said, and let it be.

What I love best about the black walnut is its bottomless, elusive taste—a brief bite of earth. I love sleep and sex, too, for advancing me toward my last passing.

AUTUMN FARM

Hotcakes on white plates, stacked for the man
in from plowing or mowing or reaping.
Stove aglow, chrome enthroned, the old woman
turns speckled suns, spatula spinning
above cast black pan, flies hovering in air.
      Who dies next?

Her worn-out man, in a curse, goes first.
The old woman waits in rooms, swatting
facet-eyed faces, her sorrow masked—
until, chair-fast, she dies without trying.

NOVEMBER MORNING

You at last wake, pushing off quilts,
leaping, in that high old way, from
your late dreams, before your body
recalls its aches, counts, out loud,
the hours until your final midnight.
You wake as morning turns to night.

And now the dogs shed their long coats,
quit their own brief lives to attend—
on slim, nimble legs, hocks cocked,
ears afloat in autumn's shrill air—
voices calling out, wild, like wolves'
across purple-painted ridges.

No remorse here. You, old wonderer,
stand into snow's needling wind,
hang on till morning, again and
again. You refuse mystery,
lay claim to hours holding their
curtained length, long-edged shadows—
for your sweet sake. It seems enough.

FROM MY ROOM, CHRISTMAS MORNING

The window outlooks a slope; trees configure glass.
Unruly as musicians or angels, they bother clouds,

flourish in their roots (though they seem dead
as winter they move, they move). A crow winds upward.

Gray strains the frame and all four sides angle east,
where the outer light shows an inner firmament:

my own walls, painted in the antique manner;
marbled columns, their capitals bearing men's faces,

benign and green, pledging renewal during sleep.
The yellow desk dictates a verged space, its legs

trees to the carpet. The chair cradles a cushion.
The clock, small-faced, accountable, frets.

On the window wall, a Kipniss lithograph: a tree,
a house, part of a sky seen through an unsheathed

opening. A bed with round knobs rests inside
the still room; its left profile seen; the right,

perceived (as spring is understood, as widows weep
alone). A plant, grizzled as the crayon that drew it,

sprays past surfaces; a drawerless chest holds another,
potted bush. Curtains gauze the windows. The bed

has no body to it. Beyond the room's sham supports
and scumbled sky, beyond the tyranny of pictures and

through the glass: sudden snow, a flurry from the roof.
At their heights the leaves of green men shine: golden,

grotesque. The bedclothes are mountainous, a hazard-
terrain. My back crushes the pillow but the headboard

resists. Nights of visions, and I am becoming bed,
I inhale wood; the sheets smell of skin, I reek of walnut.

~

I leave my sleeping place, walk over flowers stitching
summer into a woolen earth. My body tilts from

the mirror. I greet my image. I bend to Mary,
her fated morning:

> *Mary, Mary, Mother of God,*
> *what O what is true?*
> *After all, really transformed?*

NOTE: The lithograph, "Through Bedroom Curtains" is by Robert Kipniss.

WINTER NIGHT

Deer exchange deep looks
near the iced creek;
rabbits in their dumb brown line
kick, buck up
shivered green shards;
hawks' beaks glint, register
wayward moons.

The mountain's edges
face cold-dogged sun—
stones talking to wind,
voices low and obstinate.

In the house,
someone lays a fire;
another lights the cookstove.
And the curtains
close themselves against
the weighted, willful winter.

SUMMER SOLSTICE

The night
the car broke down,
summer lay on everything,
its deeps
pricked only by lightning bugs
in the tasseling corn
and the flashlight's whirling glow
on gravel.

That world has gone.
The black water
curling under the wooden bridge
has been straightened
in its banks,
the rolling road leveled.

"Oh," one of us cried, "a fox!"
And the Northern Lights
leapt,
like white fear,
all over the sky.

GIRL AND HORSE

He is there—the pinto, the enormous,
piebald pony—hoofing it by the fence,
watching the horizon that doesn't end,
the moving sky move into nothing at all.
He awaits the girl who, careful about
barbed twists, straddles the wires, then caroms
her body onto his swaying back,
seat into which she so bravely fits.

The horse starts, then rears, then bolts to the oaks—
crooked, palpable at pasture's edge—.
There he will determine if this is
the day he throws off the girl for good.

The clouds remain in their complex space;
the girl hangs on; hopes for nothing at all.

ONE SUMMER AFTERNOON

On the man-planned slope shouldering
the new highway, *foxtails grew; fronds
swaying* under the influence of cars'
spewed fumes. The grasses were
yellow-green, pale, like elvish tresses.

I stared, first at a blue chair that tilted
against my red wall—my vision careering
back, forth—until my eyes turned to
the window's shimmering, silky view.

I was blue, but why? My sky was full
of light, and the *foxtails flourished like
a changeling's hair in the hot summer ai*r.

KLEE'S "BIRD WANDERING OFF"

In an orange and strangled sky, Artist,
you strung a moon—engorged it, painted
it pink. Your white peaks graze the picture's
northern edge, in front of purple peaks.
Then, Paul, you tilted a hidebound pine—
forecasting your own tight rind? A bird, perfect

as truth, exits stiffly west, off the perfect
stair of a house or pyramid—artist,
you make us guess—and behind pines
skewed toward their black exit, darkly painted.
On Breakneck Ridge, precipitous peak
above the Hudson, the pigeon, living picture,

emerald-iridescent, aglitter, picturing
us, stepped out, one eye ruffled, perfectly
suspicious, the other calmly peeking
south, contemplating, like an artist,
the horizon. The scene was like a painting!
I offered food and the dove, pining,

captured it, flew up, an arrow into pines,
pushed forth by wind. Paul, did you picture
this? Was this what you truly painted?
Was that you, waiting at rock's perfect
edge, sheer exterior, eye glowing like an artist's,
beaked frown choking on air from high peaks?

Wasn't this continent the peaked
world you found while slowly pining
away, skin hardening like paint on your artist's
pallette? Didn't you look for pictures
in all directions, Maker, your brush sliding down perfect
mountains, the orange sky? You painted

yourself right off living's side, painted
yourself into pigment, didn't you? You peaked
early and stayed there, perfect,
breathing heightened air like a stunted pine
in a heady, breathless picture.
You made yourself into an artist,

Paul, and during your slow demise, you pined
for perfection—always conscious, Artist, picturing
peaks to paint even as you fossilized.

NOTE: Paul Klee suffered from scleroderma, a chronic skin dis-
ease marked by rigid patches of skin adhering closely to the bones.

BLUE

The beads slipped down the virgin's white slope,
precipitous crevice; flew low, like new
little birds; skimmed the blue dress's threads,
land of floating clouds—covered their glow.

They slid into the cupped palms of a pious
priest, who bedeviled them with snaking thin
digits until the gems gave in, found a child.

Love, the religious hissed, *Love*; and he draped
those beads across the child's clavicle,
down the spare and narrow chest. He fingered
the pretties; found his true god; exulted.

The child cried, and the air went quiet.
The beads glimmered on—to the next, and
the next—every innocent blinded
by his own thistled eyes and quaking lips.

GIRL ACCUSED

And if her heart were truly evil,
eyes lizard cold—
the view through the window,
the boy's mouth speaking.

Eyes lizard cold
grim on her friend's implicated arms.
The boy's mouth speaking:
Only this—he taunts,

grim on her friend's implicated arms—
No regrets! And laughs at her,
Only this, he taunts,
white teeth bared,

No regrets, and laughs at her!
Loving singly,
white teeth bared,
the girl kneels behind the knoll,

loving singly.
Brown and red leaves roil.
The girl kneels behind the knoll.
October creaks,

brown and red leaves roil.
She clutches the stolen kitchen knife.
October creaks,
her book's words bristling, instructing.

She clutches the stolen kitchen knife
as he ambles by,
her book's words bristling, instructing.
Good looking, young as love,

as he ambles by,
she *God how she hates*.
Good looking, young as love,
she tries to leave,

she *God how she hates*,
believing her life, and his.
She tries to leave.
She rises, she agonizes.

Believing her life, and his,
Retreat,
she rises, she agonizes.
Still, that honed knife, her fingers

retreat.
She can't break the circled hour.
Still, that honed knife, her fingers—
she yields to massacre.

She can't break the circled hour:
orangeyellowred.
She yields to massacre
and loses, she, her soul, this one,

orangeyellowred,
who could have been an angel,
and loses, she, her soul, this one
(they all told her)

who could have been an angel.
The wind buffeting
(they all told her),
her mother's knife gleaming.

The wind buffeting,
the mingled, winged leaves—
her mother's knife gleaming.
Why do his eyes subside like that?

The mingled, winged leaves—
shy again, she wipes him off.
Why do his eyes subside like that?—
She repeals the event. Flee.

Shy again, she wipes him off
but her hot hands conspire against her.
She repeals the event. *Flee*.
Winter, her longest season,

but her hot hands conspire against her.
And if her heart were truly evil?—
winter, her longest season;
the view through the window.

KITCHEN POEM

—for my mother

Cleaning the marble counter,
I count flaws. These gray veins
bridge shadows, startle memory—
every river lives here, every
rooted tree. The stone's low tremor
speaks of earth, calls forth
the mother of darkness. I press
my cheek to her face; stars
glimmer in her eyes. Like wind
coming to curtains, night overtakes
afternoon. My body dwindles and
ages like a kerchief, old, torn.
It flutters from forehead to eyes,
lips; I swallow myself. My mother
grieves, sings life; she pardons
all my sins while I lean, lay
the fever at her soothing door.

FROM THE MOUNTAINS

The woman said she wanted a man
who couldn't take his eyes
off her face. And then I knew
who looked at me,
whose face I longed for.

Last evening, just before
descending into Cat Hollow
on the Downsville Road, I saw clouds
that exactly matched the ridge.

Or the mountains conformed
to the clouds in the same way
Kuan Yin's still, silk coverlet
repeats the shape
of her lumbering body.

Dawn comes late
to this stony horizon. My bed
is cold. Looking for you,
I find your eyes behind
the brittle fingers of trees;
I find you, looking.

EASTER MONDAY

—to the memory of Ernest M. Fishman

Men who wear suspenders adapt
to April as if warmth
had been there for taking;
they easily discard
stiff brown coats to bend
under the hoods of cars, rake
leaves at roadside,
each man's broad back bringing
yours to me, your length, soaped:
you lean and turn while
the water pours over us
and I enter
the ellipse of your arms.

On the highway a cat, brought
forth by love, one pink ear
erect from graded macadam,
the sun filtering membrane
as if through a petal,
a portion of a rose window.

I could retreat from the line
we drew; part from you.
But you reach beyond me,
your Houdini hand cleaving tissue
as if I weren't flesh;
only illusion.

I tell you, I could be solitary
again; not allow
one hand to touch—not
the masseur's ten blind fingers
in his shuttered room,
nor your more probing ones—
no, I could be alone
this last time for all time
(but I consider your silhouette
against my easterly window,
the sun spanning the horizon,
leafless cherry trees,
blackcap briars).

I could turn back before
we rearrange the furniture to suit
(and you inside this room
with me, or I in your car,
you driving and musing, I
freely sleeping past mountains).
I am enraptured and appalled
by the homeliness of it.

Listen! Are we, any of us,
anything but brief appearances
in each others' lives? As
Gabriel to the unsuspecting Mary,
to Joseph (in that smaller,
more restrained meeting), aren't
we also miracles, we who wear
no visible wings, announce
nothing more portentous than love?

LOVE

Each night his long strong legs wrapped around hers—
trees, his rough legs. Each night his rugged hands
held her; his neck bent like a sacrifice.
That was always his way, his access—limbs
at first branching out, then going to ground,
their vast bed telling seasonal stories.
The south wind eased open rusted sashes
and the room's air escalated, contracted.

She loved it, loving him. Nor could she rise
up, withdraw to another room, even
when the tempest pushed through old panes; stayed.
(The moon, like an autumn bird, bolted clouds.)
By then, she knew, it was too late. By then—
boughs darkly entwined—holding was all.

WHEN WE WERE GHOSTS, AGAIN

I woke to you, making love to me, and
thought I loved it until I saw the wounds.
Saw your face, skin stretched taut, covert eyes,
heard your drummed words. That was enough.
But you continued, and so I watched you,
the loneliness of arms attempting embrace,
overreaching. I wanted to erase you,
our lost time, glaucous golden leaves below
October trees. But you wouldn't vanish,
wouldn't let me go. At last, heartbroken,
I wedded your lifeless shape, became—
one last time—your bodiless beloved.

VIRGINIA'S EXPLANATION

I could have moved as slowly as he,
walked the tepid pace of the getting-older,
knees forgetting function. But I did not.
Did not wait up for him; give any quarter.

I wouldn't pause, would not; no, could not lay over.
He was as if fixed, and when he mentioned flying,
all I could see was his featherless coat.
He was resistance, epitomized; dying, I knew it.

But he was also lift and calm; he was like the words
he laid down, heavy yet lighter than life, sparser than air.
Finally I had to find my own wings—
and in pocketed stones, a weightless sky.

DISCONNECT VILLANELLE

Once, I don't remember the exact day,
can't call back the lone instant—
but his words still speak, then slip away

through lips that open and sway
over white teeth; his deep voice, urgent.
Once, I don't remember the exact day

his eyes, awash in tears, gray,
were one man's closing comment.
His words still speak, then slip away.

It is as if love always meant to stray
from its sweet home, turn vagrant.
Once, I don't remember the exact day

the summer swallows flew away
and upthrust branches went silent.
But his words still speak, then slip away.

Rising up— nothing more to say—
we dusted off, divided—strange, new quotient.
Once, I don't remember the exact day.
But his words still speak, then slip away.

LET NOTHING DISTURB YOU

—St. Teresa of Avila

Fortunately women have the miraculous ability
to change the meaning of their actions after the event.

from *The Hitchhiking Game*
—MILAN KUNDERA

1.

Yes I say I still love you yes
but you can't hear me
I can't listen to you
       our speeches
              over
     plunged
          each other
grasshoppers in dry fields.

2.

Today I heard the *wind* come in.
I tracked the storm by leaves

turning their backs.
Out of the frenzy sprang a vision:

another wind, hollow eyes, hands
so strong no exertion could refute them.

(This was the first error.)

3.

I started toward the door. Just
beyond, jasmine—sweet, like the smell

in a dying room. Outside, moon-jazz:
lowdown; desperate.

I lost myself to flesh, as if I were
a painted pagan figure; I belonged

to another, weightier soul,
yet was separated by time; shape.

What we call Love is nothing;
the blanket that covers sweethearts

tears them asunder.

4.

Death. Their eyes shout it.
She holds her child's hand tightly

(she wants answers, freely given);
the little one leads her.

Trees' roots strike deep
during drought yet die from lack.

The squall's radio noise continues
but the expression on the clerk's face

does not change.

5.

Within their chambers bears *sleep*.
Again I have come to the wrong place,

like an elderly lady caught
in a busy intersection. Her

gloved shame, mine *(we, aged and
ignorant; our face sags)*.

Trapped by the future, uninvited,
I fall outside Paradise.

Animals do not remember
their plummeting, untimely deaths

from the tops of autumn trees.

6.

The moon offers half
her face. Soon she'll show

the whole unholy mask.
But now she resembles

one of those girls whose shoulders
float a *silvery shawl*;

blue paint smears her eyelids,
stars silver cheeks. She gives birth

to disorder. In the woods,
cloven rounds circle brambles—

prints in April's spurious snow.
The outcrop glimmers.

The sun grows; moon blurs.

7.

Our secrets evaded us. We
could not face our seeing; or speak.

Two vultures shift on invisible drafts.

8.

The mountain bulges, all stone,
all stone; rock thins, dangerous

as correspondence. Grasses
pattern the crust. Bruised

lowlands unfold, green and gray.
The creek sprouts islands where water

flowed. Love, love. What's the use?
I'm awash in the midnight glass;

alone, I stream toward imperfection.

Acknowledgments

2River Review: "Old January"

Anenome: "Planting Wildness"

Avatar: "Fall," "Fox on Volcán Irazú, Costa Rica"

Barrow Street: "Highway in Winter," "On the Road"

Blueline: "From the Mountains," "Sap Month," "The Cat in the Diner"

Buckle &:   "Boy with .22"

Calypso: "Savage"

Connecticut Review: "November Morning," Ravens"

Comstock Review: "Work Sestina"

Crazyquilt: "On North Mountain," "Three for Summer's End"

Dogs Singing - A Tribute Anthology (Salmon Poetry):
     "The Bitch Protests Litter Murders," "Wild, Again"

Earth's Daughters: "Walnuts"

Even the Daybreak — 35 Years of Salmon Poetry anthology (Salmon Poetry):
     "Blue Beak Speaking"

Fact-Simile: "Virginia's Explanation"

Fennel Stalk: "Summer Solstice"

First Light anthology (Calypso Press):
     "At Solstice," "First Day Rondeau"

From the Finger Lakes Poetry anthology (Cayuga Lake Books):
     "Copper Beech Trees in Winter," "The Pear Tree"

Hurricane Alice: "Closing"

Knockout: "Autumn Farm"

Leveller: "The Old Dog's Lament"

Levure Littéraire: "Fortune," "Stone and Stand," "The Day"

Like Light anthology (Bright Hill Press):
     "Treed Fisher"

Linebreak: "To the Heart"

Lucid Stone: "Wolf Moon"

Mason's Road: "Bogus"

Mudfish: "Blue Jays in September Window"

NYCBigCityLit: "Disconnet," "Luna," "Rime"

Out of the Catskills and Just Beyond Anthology (Bright Hill Press):
     "Easter Monday"

Palooka Journal: "Girl and Horse," "Love"

Paterson Literary Review:

> "What Was It Like, Losing?"

Phoebe: "Girl Accused," "Let Nothing Disturb You"

Poetry Bay: "Winter Solstice"

Poetry New York: "From My Room, Christmas Morning"

Rolling Coulter: "After Watching the Deer in the Trees"

Saranac Review: "After Blizzard Rondeau," Morning, October: The Stone Circle"

The Louisville Review: "Two in Winter"

The Enchanting Verses: "Stone Cold"

The Flutes of Power anthology (Great Elm Press):

> "Dragonfly"

The Ledge: "Vultures"

The Original Van Gogh's Anthology:

> "Blue"

The Same: "Artesian Well," "Compensation," "Dog Girl Discusses Transformation," "Hawk's Reason," "Oriole," "Season," "Southerly," "Want," "When We Were Ghosts, Again"

The Seattle Review: "Kitchen Poem"

The Second Word Thursdays Anthology (Bright Hill Press):

> "Buck"

The Wide Shore: "Holy Beast"

Wildcat: "Night and Loosestrife," "Klee's Bird Walking Off"

"Three for Summer's End" was set to music by composer Jamie Keesecker and performed at MacDowell Colony's "Music for the Mountain" Monadnock Music Festival in 2010.

"From my Room, Christmas Morning," is included in the Swetz Van Middhlar Collection of Most Beloved Poems in Manuscript, The Netherlands Literary Museum in The Hague, a department of the Royal Library of the Netherlands.

SPECIAL THANKS: I am deeply grateful to the MacDowell Colony, The Constance Saltonstall Foundation for the Arts; Hedgebrook; Hawthornden Castle International Retreat for Writers, Scotland; the Millay Colony for the Arts; The Pocantico Center/Rockefeller Brothers Fund; David and Julia White Arts Colony; the Caldera Arts Center; and Jentel Foundation for residency fellowships that gave me time and space to work on these poems. I wish also to thank Jessie Lendennie and Siobhán Hutson of Salmon Poetry for their love of and dedication to poetry.

BERTHA ROGERS, poet, translator, and visual artist, has published poems and translations in literary journals and anthologies, including the recent (which she also edited) *Like Light: 25 Years of Poetry & Prose by Bright Hill Poets &Writers* and *Even the Daybreak: 35 Years of Salmon Poetry.* Her poetry collections include *Heart Turned Back* (Salmon); *Sleeper, You Wake* (Mellen); and several chapbooks and interdisciplinary collections. Her illustrated translation of *Beowulf* was published in 2000, and her translation with illuminations of the Anglo-Saxon Riddle-Poems from the Exeter Book, *Uncommon Creatures*, was published in 2019. She has been awarded fellowships by the MacDowell Colony, Hawthornden International Writers Retreat, and others. Her writings on inclusion and cultural diversity in arts education have been published in *Open the Door*, *Education Week*, and the Poetry Foundation's *Harriet Blog.* Through Bright Hill Press & Literary Center of the Catskills, www.brighthillpress.org, a literary organization founded by Rogers and her husband, Ernest M. Fishman, in 1992, she led the development of the New York State *Literary Web Site and Literary Map* in partnership with the New York State Council on the Arts (www.nyslittree.org). She serves as Poet Laureate of Delaware County, NY; and she is a member of the selection panel for the Empire State Writers Hall of Fame.

salmonpoetry

Cliffs of Moher, County Clare, Ireland

"Like the sea-run Steelhead salmon that
thrashes upstream to its spawning ground,
then instead of dying, returns to the sea –
Salmon Poetry Press brings precious cargo
to both Ireland and America in the poetry it
publishes, then carries that select work to its
readership against incalculable odds."

TESS GALLAGHER

The Salmon Bookshop & Literary Centre

Ennistymon, County Clare, Ireland

Listed in *The Irish Times'* 35 Best Independent Bookshops